THREE LITTLE WORDS:

A, An, and The

(A Foreign Student's Guide to English Articles)

by Elizabeth Claire

illustrations by Richard Greenwood

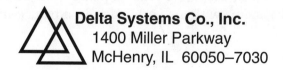

Delta Systems Co., Inc.
1400 Miller Parkway
McHenry, IL 60050–7030

ACKNOWLEDGEMENTS

Many people have helped make this book possible, and I would particularly like to thank the following: David Van Orden for his close reading of the preliminary manuscript and making numerous helpful suggestions; Terri Lehmann and Honey Wada, for suggestions on the second draft; Judy Wheeler and Seong Sook Ahn, for overseeing field-testing of the final version. I also wish to thank Esther Kim, Jun Agatsuma, Yukiko Hidaka, Dong Il Shin, Makiko Kimura, Satomi Habakari and Luz Lopez. A background of support for initiating this project was provided by the participants in the North Jersey Excellence Seminar designed by Werner Erhard.

ISBN 0-937354-46-5

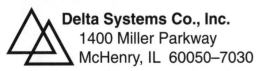 **Delta Systems Co., Inc.**
1400 Miller Parkway
McHenry, IL 60050–7030

Printed in the U.S.A.

INTRODUCTION

0.1 **The three words that are used the most often in the English language are**

0.2 *A, an,* **and** *the* **are a part of speech called** *articles.* **Whenever you see or hear an article, you can expect a** *noun* **to follow. (A noun is a word that names a person, place, thing, or idea.)**

0.3 **Sometimes the noun follows directly after** *a, an* **or** *the:*

a face

an apple

the pencil

0.4 **Sometimes there are** *adjectives* **between** *a, an* **or** *the* **and the noun. (An adjective is a word that tells about or describes a noun.)**

a happy face

an old rotten apple

the short fat pencil

1

0.5 If you leave out *a, an,* and *the,* or if you use them incorrectly, your meaning may still be clear. But it will not sound right to Americans. In some cases it can make a very big difference in the meaning of what you say.

a. He has black hair.

b. He has a black hair.

0.6 In speaking, the articles are not stressed. They are said quickly and are joined with the word that follows them. It's very hard to hear *a, an,* and *the* when Americans are talking. These little words seem to disappear!

0.7 Some languages do not have articles. In other languages there are many forms of articles and they are used in ways different from the way English uses them.

Because of these differences, almost everyone learning English has some trouble with ***a, an,*** and ***the.*** This book was written to help you.

2

HOW TO USE THIS BOOK

There are rules that can help you decide when to use *a, an,* or *the,* and when to leave them out. Each of these rules has some exceptions. And the exceptions have exceptions! Native English-speakers did not learn these rules in school. They just say "It sounds right this way."

This book has TEN STEPS to help you understand how Americans use these words. But the most important way to improve your English is to listen and read. Then the correct way will sound right to you too, when you speak and write.

If you are using this book without a teacher, here are some suggestions for you:

1. Relax. If you are nervous in conversation because of limited English, do only STEP ONE and STEP TWO in this book. Listen to native speakers as much as you can, and increase your vocabulary and understanding. Go on to the next steps only when you feel ready.

2. Ask a native-English speaker to help you with the listening and speaking parts in STEP ONE. You will need a native speaker to check some of your answers and the free composition in the mastery tests.

3. Read the rules and sentences, then do the exercises. Check your answers.

4. If you score 100 on any test, that's great! Go on to the next step.

5. If your answers do not agree with the book's answers, re-read the rules in that step. If you have more than four answers wrong, wait several days or longer before you go to the next step. Do not try to complete the book too quickly.

6. After you complete STEP NINE, take the review tests in STEP TEN and check your answers. If you have made any errors, go back to the rules. The number in parentheses tells which rule to see. For example (1.2) is paragraph 1.2 on page 5.

7. Take the MASTERY TESTS. Have a native-English speaker or a teacher correct your sentences.

8. Keep listening for the use of these three little words and notice them in your reading. Ask English-speaking friends to correct you if you are using a, an, or the incorrectly or omitting them where they are needed.

STEP ONE: Listen carefully

a man walked down the street with a small alligator on a leash!

1.1 Can you hear a, an, and the?

EXERCISE:

Train your ears to hear these little words. Listen to a native English speaker (or the teacher) read a few sentences at a time from any simple story. Make a mark (/) every time you hear **a, an** or **the.**

After each item, the reader will tell you how many times **a, an,** or **the** appeared in the sentences. Check this against the number you wrote down.

	I hear:	There really are:		I hear:	There really are:
1.	_____	_____	6.	_____	_____
2.	_____	_____	7.	_____	_____
3.	_____	_____	8.	_____	_____
4.	_____	_____	9.	_____	_____
5.	_____	_____	10.	_____	_____

Did you improve as you practiced?_____.
Practice a little every day with an English speaker reading to you.

	I hear:	There really are:		I hear:	There really are:
1.	_____	_____	6.	_____	_____
2.	_____	_____	7.	_____	_____
3.	_____	_____	8.	_____	_____
4.	_____	_____	9.	_____	_____
5.	_____	_____	10.	_____	_____

1.2 *A* and *an* mean the same thing: one.

1.3 *An* is used before words that begin with vowel sounds. (The vowels are a, e, i, o, and u.

The letter *h* is "silent" in some words.

The names of the letters *e, f, h, l, m, n, r, s,* and *x* begin with vowel sounds.

an orange	an Indian	an angry mother
an umbrella	an egg	an excellent paper
an idea	an hour	an honest person
an "f"	an "o"	an "m"
an _____	an _____	an _____

1.4 *A* is used before words that begin with consonant sounds. (Consonants are those letters which are not vowels.)

The *Eu* and *u* in some words sound like the consonant sound /yu/.

One sounds like *wun*.

The names of the letters *b, c, d, g, j, k, p, q, t, u, v, w, y,* and *z* begin with consonant sounds.

a jet	a car	a delicious hamburger
a house	a doll	a yellow submarine
a university	a unicorn	a European man
a "b"	a "t"	a one-way street
a _____	a _____	a _____

5

EXERCISES

Write *a* or *an* in the following sentences:

1. I had _____ egg for breakfast.

2. I broke _____ cup.

3. My mother bought _____ umbrella last night.

4. Betti spells her name with _____ "i", not with _____ "y".

5. After _____ hour, we got tired and went home.

6. The new student borrowed _____ ESL book from the office.

7. My teacher has _____ M.A. degree from Columbia University.

8. I would like to have _____ hundred dollars.

9. It is _____ honor to meet the governor of New Jersey.

10. My cousin joined _____ union.

11. I have never seen _____ unicorn.

12. It is good to meet _____ honest person.

13. There is _____ A & P Supermarket on the corner.

14. The word "restroom" is _____ euphemism (polite word) for toilet.

15. Ben has _____ one-track mind.

16. He goes to _____ university in California.

17. I washed my hair with _____ herbal shampoo.

18. A clown with _____ unhappy face did tricks for the children.

19. Frank has _____ unique way of looking at the world.

20. The word an is _____ article.

ANSWERS

1. an	6. an	11. a	16. a
2. a	7. an	12. an	17. an
3. an	8. a	13. an	18. an
4. an, a	9. an	14. a	19. a
5. an	10. a	15. a	20. an

1.5 There are two different ways to pronounce *the* **in careful speech. Before consonant sounds, it is pronounced** /thə/. **Listen to a native speaker say these phrases:**

the man	the Chinese puzzle	the green grass
the balloon	the red house	the long road
the bicycle	the tall woman	the difficult lesson
the union	the whole pie	the European man

1.6 Before vowel sounds, it is pronounced /thi/.

the answer	the ugly mask	the oldest fairy
the orange	the ice cream cone	the end of the story
the air	the Indian	the eighth floor
the angry girl	the open umbrella	the umpire
the "s"	the hour before dawn	the honest truth

EXERCISE:

Read the examples from groups 1.5 and 1.6 above. Practice connecting *the* with the word after it, as though the two words were just one word. Example: /thianswer/.

7

STEP TWO: Look carefully

Can you see a, an, and the?

You will learn to use the articles correctly if you become more aware of them in your reading.

EXERCISE:

A. Read this story from Aesop. Draw a circle around all the **a**'s, **an**'s and **the**'s. Count the number of words that you have circled; write that number on the line at the end of each paragraph.

THE WILD DOG AND THE FARM DOG

1. Once there was (a) wild dog who was very, very hungry. He had not had anything to eat for (a) long time. He was shaggy and thin and his bones stuck out through his skin. He ran here and there through (the) woods and meadows looking for (a) rabbit or (a) squirrel or even (a) mouse to eat. But it was winter, and he found nothing. Finally he came near (a) farm house where he met (an) old farm dog. (The) farm dog was plump and had well-brushed hair. _____9_____

2. "How come you are so plump and well-fed?" asked the wild dog. _____

3. "Oh, the farmer gives me milk, bones, and delicious scraps from his table," said the farm dog. "All I have to do is bark to warn him if robbers come; it's a very easy job. I'm sure the farmer would give you the same if you worked here too." _____

4. "I think I would like such an easy job," said the wild dog, and his mouth started to water as he thought of the milk, bones and scraps from the farmer's table. "I could protect the farm very well, as I have good ears, good eyes and a good voice. I can bark very loud." _____

5. Just then, the wild dog noticed a place around the farm dog's neck where the hair was all rubbed off. "What is that on your neck?" asked the wild dog. _____

6. "Oh, that's where my collar goes. It rubs off the hair. But it doesn't hurt; it's nothing to worry about," said the farm dog. _____

7. "Your collar? You mean you are tied up on a rope?" _____

8. "Yes, most of the time. But I don't mind," said the farm dog. "I am used to it. Let's go now so the farmer can see you and give you something to eat. You look very hungry." _____

9. "You mean you cannot run through the meadows and the woods and go wherever you please?" _____

10. "Once in a while, I wish I could," said the farm dog. "But it's no problem for me. I'm used to it. Stay. You'll get used to it too." _____

11. "No thank you," said the wild dog. "I would rather be hungry and free than well-fed on a rope. Good bye!" _____

12. And with those words, the wild dog ran off into the woods. _____

13. How many articles did you find? _____

14. Did you miss any articles? _____ How many did you miss? _____

B. Go back to the story and underline all the nouns. (A noun is the word for a person, place, thing or idea.) Notice that wherever there is an article, a noun is sure to follow. However, not all nouns have articles before them! Nouns can sometimes be used as adjectives: farm dog.

15. How many nouns did you find? _____

ANSWERS

1. 9 (see sample)
2. 1 (dog)
3. 5 (farmer, milk, bones, scraps, table, farm, dog, robbers, job, farmer)
4. 6 (job, dog, mouth, milk, bones, scraps, farmer's, table, farm, ears, eyes, voice)
5. 5 (dog, place, farm dog's neck, hair, neck dog)
6. 2 (collar, hair, farm dog)

7. 1 (collar, rope)
8. 3 (time, farm, dog, farmer)
9. 2 (meadows, woods)
10. 2 (while, farm, dog, problem)
11. 2 (dog, rope)
12. 2 (words, dog, woods)
13. 40
15. 64

10

STEP THREE: The Indefinite Article *(A/an)*

3.1 Use *a* or *an* before nouns that are singular, countable, and indefinite.

single   = one
countable = can be counted
indefinite = not definite, not specific, not previously spoken about or pointed out.

a. Would you like a cookie?

b. I ate an egg for breakfast.

3.2 Never use *a* or *an* with plural nouns or non-countable nouns. The word *some* may be used for plural indefinite or non-countable nouns.

a. I ate eggs for breakfast.   I ate some eggs for breakfast.

b. I had soup for lunch.   I had some soup for lunch.

3.3 Countable nouns are names of things that can be counted. Most (but not all) countable nouns have a definite size or shape.

one chair, two chairs, three chairs . . .
one idea   two ideas . . .
one person   two people
one deer   two deer

11

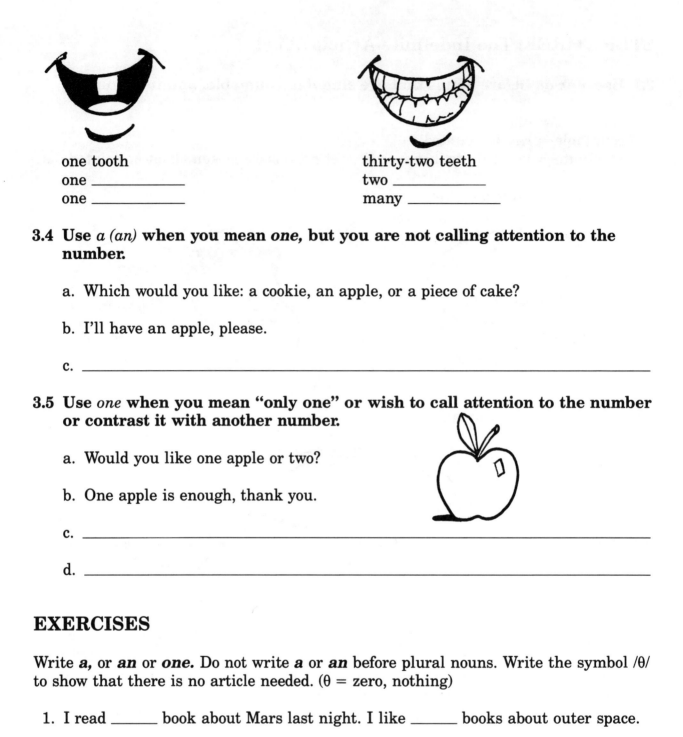

one tooth
one _____
one _____

thirty-two teeth
two _____
many _____

3.4 Use _a (an)_ when you mean _one,_ but you are not calling attention to the number.

    a. Which would you like: a cookie, an apple, or a piece of cake?

    b. I'll have an apple, please.

    c. _____

3.5 Use _one_ when you mean "only one" or wish to call attention to the number or contrast it with another number.

    a. Would you like one apple or two?

    b. One apple is enough, thank you.

    c. _____

    d. _____

EXERCISES

Write **_a,_** or **_an_** or **_one._** Do not write **_a_** or **_an_** before plural nouns. Write the symbol /θ/ to show that there is no article needed. (θ = zero, nothing)

    1. I read _____ book about Mars last night. I like _____ books about outer space.

    2. I usually read a lot, but last week, I read only _____ book.

    3. My mother baked _____ cookies yesterday. Would you like _____ cookie?

4. I used to eat two eggs and three pieces of toast for breakfast. Now I'm on a diet. For breakfast I have _____ egg and _____ piece of toast.

5. I had _____ goldfish when I was six years old. Its name was "Jaws."

6. My sister has _____ goldfish. They are always hungry.

7. Lou has two dogs, six cats and _____ parrot.

8. Joe's uncle tells _____ good stories.

9. Marc has _____ aunt who lives in Mississippi.

10. _____ old lady found _____ hungry cat.

11. We bought _____ bananas at the supermarket yesterday.

12. _____ banana was rotten, but the others were okay.

ANSWERS

1. a, θ	6. θ	11. θ
2. one	7. one (or a)	12. One
3. θ, a	8. θ	
4. one, one	9. an	
5. a	10. An a	

3.6 *Non-countable* **nouns name things that have no definite size or shape. These are also called** *mass* **nouns.**

milk	water	air
ice	oil	gravy
ice cream	butter	salt
cheese	bread	meat
coffee	jam	applesauce
ketchup	mustard	money
rain	snow	fog
chocolate	candy	gas

other mass nouns:

_____ _____ _____

_____ _____ _____

3.7 In order to show quantities of non-countable nouns, containers or units of measure must be used.

a bottle of ketchup
a cup of coffee
a dish of ice cream
a jar of mustard
a loaf of bread
a slice of bread
a nickel

a pound of butter
a quart of milk
a gallon of water
a pint of jam
a spoonful of applesauce
a grain of salt
a dollar

Other units and containers:

_____   _____

3.8 Some words can be either countable or non-countable, depending on their meaning in a sentence. When the word is countable, use *a (an);* when it is non-countable, no article is used.

a. I ate an egg for breakfast   (a whole egg)

b. I got egg on my shirt.   (an indefinite amount of egg)

c. His hair is black   (all of it.)

d. There is a hair in the soup.   (a single strand of hair)

e. Do you want chicken?   (the meat of a chicken)

f. Do you want a chicken?   (a whole bird)

g. Mary had a little lamb.   (a baby sheep, a pet)

h. Sarah ate lamb for dinner.   (meat from a lamb)

i. a fish = the whole animal

j. fish = the meat from a fish

k. candy = a kind of food

l. a candy = one piece of candy

EXERCISES

Write **a** only where it is needed. Write θ where no article is needed.

1. Do you want _____ milk with your coffee?

2. I like _____ lamb, especially with potatoes and lots of gravy.

3. Henry has _____ lamb. Its name is "Snow White."

4. We always have _____ bread with our meals.

5. Put _____ salad dressing on your salad.

6. The mechanic put _____ quart of oil into the engine.

7. We found _____ money on the sidewalk.

8. Where can I buy _____ meat?

9. Can you give me _____ bowl of rice?

10. _____ grain of salt is very small.

ANSWERS

1. θ		6. a	
2. θ		7. θ	
3. a		8. θ	
4. θ		9. a	
5. θ		10. a	

16

STEP FOUR: Other uses of *a* and *an*

4.1 Use *a* or *an* when you are telling that someone has a certain job or occupation.

    a. My father is a banker.

    b. Joe is a truck driver.

    c. Can he be a singer with such an awful voice?

    d. Louis is studying to be an engineer.

    e. Carmen is a very good cook.

    f. _____

    g. _____

4.2 Use *a* or *an* in expressions of time or measurement.

    a. We have gym three times a week.

    b. She goes to California twice a year.

    c. I visit my grandmother once a month.

    d. Joe earns two dollars an hour.

    e. Those shoes cost thirty dollars a pair.

    f. Butter is a dollar seventy a pound now.

    g. The car was speeding at seventy miles an hour.

    h. _____

    i. _____

4.3 Use *a* or *an* in these common expressions:

    a. I saw him a couple of months ago.

    b. All of a sudden, the engine began to shake and rattle.

    c. It's been a long time since I saw you.

d. Did you have a good time?

e. I'm in a hurry to get to my class.

f. As a matter of fact, we agree with you completely.

g. It's a shame it rained during your whole vacation.

h. What a pity that she lost her job, her husband and her best friend.

i. Charlie is always in a good mood after he has a good dinner.

j. New Yorkers always seem to be in a rush.

k. _____

4.4 Do not use *a (an)* in expressions with "kind of," "type of" or "sort of."

a. Florida is the kind of place I like to visit.
b. Mary is the sort of daughter who makes parents happy to have children.
c. Henry is the type of person you trust immediately.
d. _____

4.5 Few / *a few*   little / *a* little

Here are cases where the word ***a*** completely changes the meaning of a sentence:

a. Jack has few friends. He is often lonely. (few = not many, almost none)

b. John has a few friends in New York. He visits them whenever he goes there. (a few = several, 3, 4, 5, etc.)

c. Joe has quite a few friends. There were fifty people at his birthday party. (quite a few = many, an impressive number)

d. Nancy has little money. She can't afford a vacation this year. (little = not much; a very small quantity; not enough)

e. Nicky has very little money. He had to borrow two hundred dollars from his father to help pay the rent. (very little = almost none)

f. Maria has a little money. She's going to Florida for a vacation. (a little = some, enough)

g. _____

h. _____

4.6 Other expressions with *a*

a. **A great many** people marched in the parade.

b. **A good many of** my ideas come to me in my dreams.

c. **A good number of** students attend regularly.

d. Chang sends **a great deal of** his money to his parents back in Taiwan.

e. **Many a** foreign student has been confused by English grammar.
= Many foreign students have been confused by English grammar.

EXERCISES

Write *a, an,* or *one,* or θ in the lines:

1. Eggs cost ninety cents _____ dozen.

2. We eat three times _____ day.

3. Joe saw her _____ couple of months ago.

4. If you're in _____ hurry, I can get it for you now.

5. Would you like _____ sugar in your tea?

6. Jack caught _____ fish.

7. Paul ate _____ fish for dinner last night.

8. Are you in _____ good mood?

19

9. The speed limit is fifty-five miles _____ hour.

10. His uncle is _____ teacher.

11. Carlos wants to be _____ astronaut.

12. Is this the kind of _____ party you like?

13. _____ few people like to admit that they are wrong. (Not many people)

14. There were _____ few people at the party last night. (Several people)

15. If you have _____ little time, I can tell you the story. (a small amount of time)

16. She has _____ little energy. She's always tired. (Not much energy)

17. Read a page of your usual reading material and underline **a** and **an** wherever they appear. Notice the nouns that follow. See if they are countable nouns, or nouns that are in the common expressions you just read about.

18. Make a tape recording of an English talk show, commercial or news broadcast. Listen to it several times until you can clearly hear the articles and identify the nouns that follow them.

ANSWERS

1. a	6. a,	11. an
2. a	7. θ	12. θ
3. a	8. a	13. θ
4. a	9. an	14. a
5. θ	10. a	15. a
		16. θ

How are you doing so far?

STEP FIVE: The Definite Article *(the)*

5.1 **The word *the* points out a definite person, place or thing or idea, or one that has been mentioned before. (mention = talk about, refer to)**
The may be used with either singular or plural nouns.

a. I liked the story in STEP TWO about the wild dog and the farm dog.

b. The exercises in this book will help us to use the articles correctly.

c. _____

d. _____

5.2 **Use *the* when the listener or reader already knows which things you mean, or when there is only one possible item you are speaking about.**

a. I took the cat to the veterinarian. (my cat, or the cat I usually talk about; the only veterinarian in town, or the usual veterinarian I go to) (veterinarian = animal doctor)

Compare: I took a cat to a veterinarian. (It is not certain which cat or which veterinarian the speaker is talking about.)

b. I took the car to the repair shop to have the brakes fixed. (the speaker's car or the car the speaker has talked about before; the repair shop the speaker usually goes to or has talked about before, or the only repair shop in town; the brakes that are on the car)

Compare: I bought a car from a repair shop. (A car and a repair shop that the speaker has not spoken about before.)

c. The family that lives in apartment 5B comes from Hong Kong. (*The* is used because there is an explanation that makes it clear (definite) which family I am talking about. There is only one family that lives in apartment 5B.

Compare: A family that lives on Main Street comes from Singapore. (There are many families that live on Main Street, so it is still not clear to you which one.)

21

d. Could you lend me the green marker please? (There is only one possible green marker.)

Compare: Could you lend me a green marker please? (Any green marker will do, and there may be more than one.)

e. _____

f. _____

EXERCISES

Write **a** or **the** in the following sentences:

1. Once upon a time, there was _____ wild dog.

2. He came to _____ farm and met _____ farm dog.

3. _____ wild dog spoke to _____ farm dog about his job.

4. _____ job was easy; all _____ farm dog had to do was bark if _____ robber came near _____ farm.

5. _____ farmer fed _____ farm dog milk, bones and scraps from _____ family's dinner table.

6. _____ wild dog saw _____ mark on _____ farm dog's neck.

7. _____ mark was from _____ rope.

8. "Goodbye," said _____ wild dog.

9. He did not want to wear _____ rope around his neck.

10. _____ farm dog was sad to see him leave.

11. I needed _____ new rain coat.

12. I went to _____ new clothing store on Main Street.

13. _____ saleslady in _____ coat department was very helpful.

14. I wanted _____ short coat, but couldn't find one.

15. _____ saleslady showed me where _____ short rain coats were.

16. I bought _____ light blue rain coat, and _____ light blue hat to match.

17. _____ coat was sixty dollars and _____ hat was ten.

ANSWERS

1. a	11. a
2. a, a	12. the (a)
3. the, the	13. A (the)
4. The, the, a, the	14. a
5. the, the, the	15. the
6. The, a, the	16. a, a
7. The, a	17. The, the
8. the	
9. a	
10. The	

5.3 Use *the* with things that are the only ones of their kind. (There may be others in the same class of things, but we don't usually think about them.)

a. The sun rose at six a.m. this morning. (the sun in our solar system.)

b. The moon and the stars shone brightly last night. (our moon, and the stars we ordinarily see at night.)

c. Have you read the Bible? (the famous Christian collection of stories)

d. The sky is blue. (today's sky or the usual sky above us.)

e. The weather is great. (our present weather)

f. The world is full of opportunities. (our world.)

g. Forget about the past. (the time before today)

h. Don't worry about the future. (the time after today)

i. There is no time like the present. (now)

j. I spoke to him on the telephone yesterday.

k. I heard about it on the radio.

l. In just two minutes we'll be on the air. (broadcasting over the radio)

m. In just two minutes we'll be in the air. (flying in the Earth's atmosphere)

n. (Notice: I saw it on television last night.)

o. _____

p. _____

EXERCISE:

Write **a, an** or **the** only where they are needed. Write θ where nothing is needed.
  1. How is _____ weather in Puerto Rico in the summer?

2. I love looking at _____ ocean.

3. _____ future will be here before you know it.

4. My favorite book is _____ Bible.

5. Barry found _____ wallet that everyone had been looking for.

6. Carrie found _____ wallet in the subway. (one she hadn't known about before)

7. During an eclipse of _____ sun, the shadow of _____ moon falls on _____ earth.

8. What do you think about _____ economy?

9. Don't let _____ past run your life.

10. Do you listen to _____ radio in your car on your way to work?

11. What did you watch on _____ TV last night?

12. You ought to see _____ doctor. (any doctor)

13. You ought to see _____ doctor. (your doctor)

14. I bought _____ new suit and _____ hat to match.

15. _____ moon is 240,000 miles from _____ earth.

16. Sometimes you can see _____ planet Venus in the west, just after _____ sun sets.

17. I saw _____ shooting star last night.

ANSWERS

1. the	6. a	11. θ	16. the, the
2. the	7. the, the, the	12. a	17. a
3. The	8. the	13. the	
4. The	9. the	14. a, a	
5. the	10. the	15. The, the	

5.4 When something is outstanding, or excellent in comparison with others of its kind, we stress the word _the_ before it. In writing, we usually underline it or write it in italic letters. In speaking, it is often pronounced /thi/.

a. Sherry gave _the_ party of the year.

b. I met *the* man last night. (The speaker is saying that this man is very special; he is "Mr. Right." (i.e. someone to fall in love with and marry)

5.5 Always use *the* with superlatives:

a. She is the best cook I have ever known.

b. That's the best picture in the whole museum.

c. Dick bought the most expensive watch in the store.

d. I buy nothing but the best for my family

e. _____

f. _____

EXERCISES

Write *the,* or *a (an)* in the following sentences.

1. Bill is _____ nice person. He is _____ nicest person I have ever met.

2. I just read _____ interesting book. It was _____ most interesting book in the whole library.

3. Mother bought _____ expensive dress. In fact, it was _____ most expensive dress in the store.

4. Mother said that _____ best thing to do for the flu is go to bed and rest.

5. _____ good thing to do for a headache is to put ice on your forehead.

6. Last winter was _____ worst winter in twenty years.

7. Maggie is _____ prettiest girl in the class.

8. One of _____ most difficult things to master in English is the use of articles.

ANSWERS

1. a, the
2. an, the
3. an, the
4. the

5. A (one)
6. the
7. the
8. the

26

STEP SIX: The Definite Article versus the Indefinite Article

6.1 Use the definite article, *the,* **when you want to point something out and make it definite.**

(*The* is like **this**, **that**, **these** and **those** except that it does not show place, and it may be used with either singular and plural nouns.)

Use the indefinite article *a (an),* **with singular nouns that are not definite.**

The plural form for the indefinite article *(a, an)* **is** *no* **article.** (θ)

a. Definite: The boys in Richard's class are athletes. (those boys)

b. Indefinite: Boys grow up to be men. (any boys, all boys)

c. Definite: The teachers at this school are kind. (these teachers)

d. Indefinite: Teachers need special training. (any teachers, all teachers)

e. Definite: _____

f. Indefinite: _____

EXERCISES

Write *the* only with definite nouns. Write θ for plural, indefinite nouns:

1. It's hot in this room. Can you open _____ windows?

2. _____ girls mature faster than _____ boys.

3. Do you think _____ dogs are smarter than _____ cats?

4. Where are _____ girls you told me about?

5. _____ scientists I spoke to are working on a way to create cheaper electricity.

6. Mother says that _____ vegetables are good for you.

7. _____ vegetables from my garden are nice and fresh.

ANSWERS

1. the
2. θ, θ
3. θ, θ
4. the

5. The
6. θ
7. The

6.2 Do not use *the* with months, days of the week, or holidays.

a. I'll see you in April.

b. Wednesday comes before Thursday.

c. Lou's birthday is August 12.

d. There are only 10 days till Christmas.

e. My family always enjoys Thanksgiving.

f. New Year's Day falls on (a) Monday this year.

6.3 Exceptions: Use *the* in expressions such as "the Fourth of July."

a. My birthday is the twelfth of January.

6.4 When days of the week are modified by a following phrase, use *the*.

a. We can leave work a half hour early the Friday before vacation.

b. "Mardi Gras" is the Tuesday before Lent begins.

6.5 Do not use *the* before personal names.

a. Joe is my friend.

b. Mrs. Baffa is a principal.

c. I saw Senator Chase.

d. King George signed the treaty.

e. _____

f. _____

6.6 Exception: When there is more than one person by the same name, use *the* **to make it clear which one you mean.**

    a. The John Brown from Los Angeles is the one I was talking about, not the John Brown from San Francisco.

    b. _____

6.7 When you refer to all the people in a family, use *the* **and the plural form of the family name.**

    a. The Lopezes live in Fort Lee.

    b. All the Katos had the flu last winter.

    c. Have you seen the Foxes lately?

    d. _____

6.8 Another way to refer to the entire family is to use *the* **plus the family name, plus the word family.**

    a. There have been many famous people in the Kennedy family.

    b. _____

6.9 *The* **is used with some proper names followed by an adjective or noun:**

Alexander the Great	Jimmy the Greek
Richard the Lionhearted	William the Conqueror
Louis XIV (Louis the Fourteenth)	Leif the Lucky
Elizabeth II (Elizabeth the Second)	Eric the Red

EXERCISES

Write *the* only where it is necessary in the following sentences:

1. Where is _____ Betsy?

2. Frances married _____ Dr. Smith who is a surgeon, not _____ Dr. Smith who is a dentist.

3. _____ Dr. Jonas Salk created a vaccine for polio.

4. _____ Wongs moved after they won the lottery.

5. Do you know _____ Browns?

6. _____ Mr. Brown is my best friend.

7. _____ Trump family went on vacation last week.

8. This course was taught by _____ Professor Wheeler last year.

9. Have you ever heard of John _____ Baptist?

10. Who was Alfred _____ Great's son?

11. _____ Halloween is in _____ October.

12. We worked hard on _____ Monday and _____ Tuesday, but we played _____ Wednesday.

13. His birthday is on _____ Fourth of July.

14. We celebrated _____ New Year's Eve quietly at home.

15. _____ Wednesday before _____ Thanksgiving is a busy day for the family cook.

ANSWERS

1. θ	6. θ	11. θ, θ
2. the, the	7. The	12. θ, θ, θ
3. θ	8. θ	13. the
4. The	9. the	14. θ
5. the	10. the	15. The, θ

6.10 When talking about clothing or parts of the body, a personal adjective pronoun (my, your, his, her, our, etc.) is often used. (not the definite article as in some other languages)

a. My stomach aches.

b. She cut her finger.

c. Fix your tie.

d. There is a hole in your shirt.

e. We worked until our arms ached.

f. The dog used his nose to find the robber.

g. The cat knocked over the glass with its tail.

h. _____

6.11 Exceptions:

I have a headache, a toothache, a stomachache, a back ache.

Use **the** with parts of the body after *myself, himself, yourself,* etc. In phrases after *on, in, over* and *by* showing the location of an action received by the owner of the body part, either **the** or a personal adjective pronoun may be used.

a. Carry bumped herself on the head.

b. He cut himself on the thumb.

c. The victim was shot in the chest.   (or, in his/her chest)

d. The teacher pulled the boy by the ear.   (or, by his ear)

e. The stone hit her in the shoulder.   (or, in her shoulder)

f. The soldier was wounded in the leg.   (or, in his leg)

g. The baby pulled the cat by the tail.   (or, by its tail)

h. Compare: The ball went over his head.
              He was hit over the head.

6.12 Do not use *the* with certain other "noun markers." Some of these are:

this	my	another	much
that	your	every	no
these	her	some	
those	his	any	
whose	its	either	
which	our	neither	
what	their	enough	

EXERCISES

Write ***the*** or ***a (an)*** or a personal pronoun adjective (*my your, her, his, our,* etc.) where they are needed.

1. Janet brushed _____ hair.

2. Richard hurt himself in _____ shoulder.

3. We washed _____ hands in hot water.

4. The boy cut himself on _____ leg.

5. She had _____ toothache all night long.

6. I hurt _____ back.

7. The old man bumped _____ head.

8. Did the old man bump himself on _____ head?

9. The policeman shot the robber in _____ back.

10. She grabbed him by _____ neck and shook him.

ANSWERS

1. her	6. my
2. the	7. his
3. our	8. the
4. the	9. the
5. a	10. the

STEP SEVEN: Using *the* with mass nouns and abstract nouns

7.1 *Mass nouns* are *non-countable* nouns that have no definite size or shape. (See 3.6) Here are some additional mass nouns.

air	dirt	rice	sugar	weather
cloth	dust	soap	chalk	sunshine
garbage	food	soup	oatmeal	moonlight
paper	furniture	metal	pork	mayonnaise
land	grass	iron	tea	gold

other mass nouns:

_____   _____   _____

7.2 **Do not use any article when talking about the *entire category* of a mass noun. (Even if there is an adjective before the noun.)**

a. Water is composed of hydrogen and oxygen.

b. Butter is fattening.

c. We need air to breathe.

d. Paper is made from wood pulp.

e. I like chocolate milk.

f. Colombian coffee is expensive.

g. _____

h. _____

7.3 **Use *the* when you are talking about a specific example or portion of the mass.**

a. The water from this fountain is cold.

b. The love of a dog is reliable.

c. The butter in this dish is melting.

d. The air in this room is hard to breathe.

e. _____

f. _____

EXERCISES

Write *the* where it is necessary:

1. _____ cheese is made from _____ milk.

2. _____ milk that you bought yesterday is sour.

3. _____ air at Mount Washington is cold, fresh and clean.

4. _____ gold is used to make jewelry.

5. _____ silver from that mine is a very high quality.

6. I want to make a sandwich. Where's _____ butter?

7. This house is full of _____ dust.

8. _____ dust in this house is two inches deep!

9. There is no shortage of _____ oil this year.

10. _____ ketchup in this bottle won't pour out.

11. _____ ketchup is made from tomatoes.

12. _____ coffee contains caffeine.

13. _____ Brazilian coffee is less expensive than Colombian coffee.

14. _____ coffee in this pot is too strong.

15. _____ ice is frozen water.

16. _____ ice on our lake was 18 inches thick last winter.

ANSWERS

1. θ, θ	5. The	9. θ	13. θ
2. The	6. the	10. The	14. The
3. The	7. θ	11. θ	15. θ
4. θ	8. The	12. θ	16. The

7.4 An abstract noun is a word that names a non-tangible thing or idea, such as emotions, qualities or actions. (Non-tangible = does not have a physical body; can not be touched.)

34

These are examples of abstract nouns:

beauty	fear	disease	space
truth	freedom	small pox	war
love	slavery	nature	work
marriage	history	religion	music
murder	hunger	science	time
friendship	art	health	photography
poetry	peace	mathematics	anger
education	literature	English	courage

other abstract nouns:

_____   _____   _____

7.5 Use *the* when the noun "belongs" to a particular person, group, or place.

a. Mr. and Mrs. Jones were happy about the marriage of their son.

b. The War Between the States was fought from 1861–1865.

c. Amy is studying the history of Japan.

d. _____

7.6 Do not use *the* when the abstract noun includes the entire category it refers to.

a. Mr. Smith doesn't believe in marriage. (any marriage, or all marriage)

b. War is horrible. (any war)

c. History is a fascinating subject. (any or all history)

d. _____

7.7 The name of a language, a school subject or field of study usually does not use the word *the* unless it is restricted, or belongs to a particular person or place.

a. He speaks French.

b. The French spoken in Quebec is different from the French spoken in Paris.

c. We studied literature last year.

d. Professor Jones teaches a course on the literature of the Middle Ages.

e. _____

f. _____

EXERCISES

Write *the* where it is needed in these sentences:

1. I am going to study _____ Spanish next year.

2. _____ death is not always sad.

3. The children were sad about _____ death of their cat.

4. I think _____ history of the United States is very interesting.

5. Many visitors to the United States were surprised by _____ kindness of Americans.

6. Children should learn _____ courtesy in school.

7. Do you like _____ poetry?

8. I like _____ poetry of the eighteenth century.

9. Marie appreciated _____ friendship of her classmate Anna.

10. _____ time flies.

11. We all enjoy _____ beauty.

12. He was greatly moved by _____ beauty of the sunset.

13. We enjoy _____ literature.

14. _____ literature of ancient Greece is still worth reading.

15. _____ space between the wall and the sofa was narrow.

16. Men have traveled in _____ space.

17. My favorite subjects at school were _____ English, _____ science, _____ gym, and _____ math.

ANSWERS

1. θ	7. θ	12. the
2. θ	8. the	13. θ
3. the	9. the	14. The
4. the	10. θ	15. The
5. the	11. θ	16. θ
6. θ		17. θ, θ, θ, θ

7.8 Generally, no *the* is used with words for diseases.

arthritis	tuberculosis	polio
cancer	sinus trouble	diphtheria
high blood		
pressure	scarlet fever	appendicitis
rheumatism	heart disease	
AIDS	leukemia	

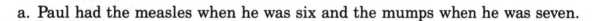

   a. He suffered from arthritis, heart disease and diabetes for most of his later
      life.

   b. Children must be protected against diphtheria and whooping cough.

7.9 Exceptions

a cold   an allergy
a fever   a tumor
a bad heart
a broken leg (arm, finger, bone, etc.)
a headache, toothache, backache, stomachache, etc.
the measles   the chicken pox
the mumps   the "willies"

   a. Paul had the measles when he was six and the mumps when he was seven.

   b. I have an allergy to tomatoes.

   c. Loud noise gives me a headache.

   d. The doctors removed a tumor from his stomach.

   e. I get "the willies" when I walk past a dark cemetery at night.

7.10 Use *the* after *study, practice* and *play* for *musical instruments.*

   a. Joe is studying the violin.

   b. Can you play the piano?

   c. She had to practice the trumpet
      two hours a day.

   d.

7.11 Don't use *the* **before** *school subjects, sports* **or** *games.*

a. We played baseball all afternoon.

b. Jack studied mathematics for years.

c. She beat me at checkers.

d. _____

EXERCISES

Write *the* or *a* where they are needed. Write θ where no article is needed.

1. Can Mary play _____ football?

2. I know how to play _____ chess.

3. Does your sister play _____ guitar?

4. No, she is studying _____ French horn, but she doesn't play it very well.

5. Bill is going to play _____ ping pong after school.

6. Jack plays _____ drums with a famous rock group.

7. When I go to college I am going to study _____ music.

8. Have you ever had _____ mumps?

9. My grandfather had _____ bad heart and _____ arthritis.

10. The doctors treated him for _____ high blood pressure.

ANSWERS

1. θ	5. θ	8. the
2. θ	6. the	9. a, θ
3. the	7. θ	10. θ
4. the		

7.12 "Object-activity words"

Object-activity words are words that can have two related, but different meanings. One meaning of the word is an object (or building). The other meaning is the activity that is connected with that object or building.

bed	school	college	class	church
jail	prison	court	town	vacation

Use _the_ when only the object or building is meant.

Don't use _the_ when you include the activity that goes on in the object or at the building.

a. The bed in my room is comfortable. (_the_ is used because only the physical bed is meant.)

b. I go to bed at ten o'clock. (_The_ is not used because bed here means both an object and the activity that takes place in the object: resting or sleeping.)

c. The English class I go to is for international students.

d. We are studying about articles in English class.

EXERCISE

Notice the differences between the following sentences. Can you understand why _the_ is used in some places and not in others?

1. School begins at nine o'clock.

2. The school I go to is on Anderson Avenue.

3. The criminal went to prison.

4. The prison is near the Hudson River.

5. My friend goes to church every Sunday.

6. Where is the church?

7. My older brother is at college.

8. I'll meet you in front of the college at nine o'clock.

9. Don't sit on the bed.

10. Our niece goes to bed at seven o'clock.

11. She took her ex-husband to court.

12. We met in front of the court.

13. _____

14. _____

STEP EIGHT: When to use *the* with place names and directions

8.1 Use *no* article for names of continents, countries, cities, states, counties, mountains, lakes, islands, beaches, streets, avenues, parks, Heaven, hell, and Paradise.

- a. Asia and Africa are continents.
- b. Boston is in Massachusetts.
- c. Bergen County is in New Jersey.
- d. Mount Everest is in Asia.
- e. Puerto Rico and Hispaniola are islands.
- f. We walked from Washington Square up Fifth Avenue to Central Park.
- g. Lake Erie is between New York State and Canada.
- h. Lizzy dreamed she was in Paradise.
- i. _____
- j. _____

8.2 Use *the* with groups of islands or lakes, and mountain ranges, or names with plural forms.

- a. The Philippines were named after Philip II of Spain.
- b. Cuba is known as "the Pearl of the Antilles."
- c. The Great Lakes are far from the Rocky Mountains.
- d. Another name for Holland is the Netherlands.
- e. The Andes Mountains are higher than the Alps.
- f. The Azores are near the Canary Islands.
- g. Many alligators live in The Everglades.
- h. _____

8.3 Use *the* with names containing Union, United, Kingdom, Republic, Empire, or Dynasty.

the Soviet Union
the U.S.S.R.
the United States
the United Arab Republic

the Kingdom of Sweden
the People's Republic of China
the Roman Empire
the Han Dynasty

8.4 Certain city names contain *the.*

The Hague   the Bronx

8.5 Some nicknames of cities contain *the*

"the Big Apple"   "the City of Brotherly Love"

8.6 Names of streets, when followed by a phrase with "of" use *the:*

the Avenue of the Americas

8.7 Use *the* **with deserts, peninsulas, oceans, seas, gulfs, rivers, canals, bridges, tunnels, zoos, and gardens.**

    a. The Sahara is a huge desert, bigger than the Mojave.
    b. The Red Sea separates Egypt from Israel and Saudi Arabia.
    c. The George Washington Bridge crosses the Hudson River.
    d. Cars can also cross via the Lincoln Tunnel or the Holland Tunnel.
    e. Children love the Bronx Zoo but are sometimes bored with the Botanical Gardens.
    f. The Mississippi and the Amazon are the two largest rivers in the world, while the Nile is the longest.
    g. _____

8.8 Use *the* **with North, South, East, and West when they are used to refer to a section of the country or of the world.**

    a. The Civil War was fought between the North and the South.

    b. The Northeast is more densely populated than the Southwest.

    c. _____

Use *the* **with north, south, east and west after a prepositional phrase.**

    d. The United States is bounded by the Atlantic Ocean on the east, the Pacific Ocean on the west, and the Gulf of Mexico on the south.

    e. _____

8.9 When north, south, east and west are used as single word adverbs, do not use *the*.

a. The explorer looked east, then west. He tested the wind and decided to continue north.

b. New York is south of Boston.

c. California is west of Nevada.

d. _____

8.10 Colleges, schools and universities: Use *the* if the name of the school is followed by a phrase beginning with *of* or *for*:

the University of Southern California   the College of William and Mary
the City College of New York   the School for the Blind

_____   _____

Do not use *the* if there is no phrase following the name of the school.

Rutgers State University   Columbia University
Notre Dame   Harvard
Northwestern University   Yale

_____   _____

Do not use *the* if you use the initials only of the school.

a. I graduated from C.C.N.Y., but my brother went to U.C.L.A.

b. _____

8.11 Use *the* with names of buildings

the Museum of Natural History   the Holiday Inn
the Smithsonian   the Jefferson Memorial
the Gallery of Modern Art   the White House
the Empire State Building   the World Trade Center

_____   _____

Exceptions: Names of buildings with Hall, Hospital do not use *the.* **Some buildings with House do not use** *the.*

  a. The name of her dormitory was Archer Hall.

  b. Valley Hospital is in Westwood; University Hospital is in Manhattan.

  c. Blair House is in Washington, D.C.

EXERCISES

1. We saw _____ Eiffel Tower when we were in _____ Paris.

2. Last year, I took a course at _____ University of Miami in _____ Florida.

3. _____ Canada is _____ north of _____ United States.

4. _____ Lake Superior is one of _____ Great Lakes.

5. We went to _____ Bahamas for our vacation.

6. _____ New York City is also known as "_____ Big Apple."

7. Have you ever climbed _____ Mount Washington?

8. Boats can go from _____ Albany to _____ Buffalo using _____ Mohawk River and _____ Barge Canal.

9. _____ English Channel separates _____ Great Britain and _____ France.

10. _____ Brooklyn Bridge goes over _____ East River.

11. I love _____ Central Park. It's bounded by _____ Fifth Avenue on _____ east, and _____ Central Park West on _____ west.

12. _____ Southwest is called "The Sun Belt."

ANSWERS

1. the, θ
2. the, θ
3. θ, θ, the
4. θ, the
5. the
6. θ, The

7. θ
8. θ, θ, the, the
9. The, θ, θ
10. The, the
11. θ, θ, the, θ, the
12. The

STEP NINE: Other rules and exceptions

9.1 Do not use *the* with most names of businesses.

Macy's	Saks Fifth Avenue
Bloomingdales	Ford
Con Edison	New Jersey Bell
Black and Tan Buses	Jeffrey's Repair Shop
IBM	

9.2 Exceptions: When the last word in the company name is company, *the* is sometimes used.

the Bridgetown Lumber Company
the Ford Motor Company
the A & P (the Atlantic and Pacific Tea Company)

9.3 About 80% of magazines do not use *the* with their titles:

Discovery	Ebony
Playboy	TV Guide
Ms.	Time
Scientific American	Newsweek
Reader's Digest	Better Homes and Gardens

But:

the Quarterly Review
the Saturday Evening Post
the New Yorker

9.4 Most newspapers have the word *the* in their titles:

The New York Times   The Daily News
The Post   The Campus Reporter
The Washington Post   The Wall Street Journal

_____

a. When I got home, the first thing I did was read The Post.

b. Would you get me The Times while you are at the store?

c. _____

9.5 Use *the* with the names of periods of history (ages, years, and centuries) and the names of wars, battles, agreements, treaties, and alliances.

the Golden Age of Greece   the Stone Age
the Pax Romana   the Industrial Revolution
the American Revolution   the Grand Alliance
the Middle Ages   the nineteen eighties
the twelfth century   the Roaring Twenties
the Renaissance

_____   _____

Exceptions:

World War One   World War Two

9.6 Use *the* with ordinal numbers before a noun. (ordinal numbers = first, second, third, fourth, etc.)

(Next and last are sometimes used like ordinal numbers. In these cases, use the.

a. The first person to arrive was Mr. Hendricks.

b. The second person was Mrs. Smally.

c. We live on the fourth floor.

d. The last month of the year is December.

e. Sharon ate too much on her birthday. The next day she was sick.

f. _____

g. _____

9.7 Next/last + year, week, month, holiday or season: If the point of time you are starting from is *now*, do not use *the*.

    a. Next year we are going to the mountains for vacation.

    b. Last week our company sold three thousand widgets.

    c. I hope we can come to visit you next summer.

    d. We had a good time last New Year's Eve.

    e. _____

    f. _____

9.8 Do not use *the* with certain phrases with ordinal numbers.

    a. It was love at first sight.

    b. At first glance, it looked like the right one.

    c. On second thought, his idea seems quite useful.

9.9 When a number follows a noun, do not use *the*.

    a. I read Chapter Nine and Chapter Eight for homework.

    b. The plane departs from Gate Four.

    c. _____

9.10 Use *the* for names of sports teams, groups, organizations and government departments

the American Red Cross	the fire department
the New York Mets	the police
the Philharmonic Orchestra	the board of education
the town council	the United States Senate
the House of Representatives	the I.R.S.

EXERCISES

Write *the* where it is needed. Write θ where no article is needed.

1. _____ General Motors is one of America's largest companies.

2. Do you shop at _____ Bloomingdales?

3. His favorite magazines are _____ Scientific American and _____ Playboy.

4. _____ Washington Post is a famous newspaper.

5. We studied about _____ American Revolution in history class.

6. Many people were killed in _____ Second World War.

7. Are you going to school _____ next week?

8. _____ last time I saw her, she was a blonde.

9. Today is May first. _____ last month was April.

10. I was planning to go to his party, but on _____ second thought, I changed my mind.

11. Her bus leaves from _____ Platform Sixty-two.

12. Call _____ police!

ANSWERS

1. θ	7. θ
2. θ	8. The
3. θ, θ	9. θ
4. The	10. θ
5. the	11. θ
6. The	12. the

STEP TEN: Review exercises

Take each test and check your answers. If you have any errors, review the rules indicated by the numbers in parentheses.

REVIEW EXERCISE ONE: CONCEPTS

Complete these sentences:

1. The three words used most often in the English language are _____ , _____ and _____ . (0.1)

2. These three words are a part of speech called _____ . (0.2)

3. A noun is a word that names a _____ , _____ , _____ or _____ . (0.2)

4. Whenever you see or hear **a, an** or **the,** you can expect a _____ to follow. (0.2)

5. The word **a** or **an** means _____ . (1.2)

6. **An** is used before words that begin with _____ sounds. (1.3)

7. The indefinite article _____ is used before words that begin with consonant sounds. (1.4)

8. The word **the** is pronounced in two different ways, _____ before consonant sounds, and _____ before vowel sounds. (1.5, 1.6)

9. The indefinite (not definite, not previously mentioned) articles are _____ and _____ . (3)

10. The definite article is _____ . (5)

11. Boy chair, star, foot are examples of _____ (countable, non-countable) nouns. (3.3)

12. Non-countable nouns name things that have no definite size or shape. These are also called _____ nouns. (3.6)

ANSWERS

1. a, an, the
2. articles
3. person, place
   thing or idea
4. noun
5. one
6. vowel

7. a
8. /thə/, /thi/
9. a, an
10. the
11. countable
12. mass

Number correct: _____ out of 19.

REVIEW EXERCISE TWO

Write **a** or **an** only where they are needed. Write θ where no article is needed.

1. I ate _____ orange this morning. (1.3, 3.1)

2. The man drove the wrong way down _____ one-way street. (1.4, 3.1)

3. Do you spell your name with _____ "s" or _____ "z?" (1.3, 1.4)

4. We had to wait _____ hour for dinner. (1.3, 3.1)

5. We ordered _____ lamb for our meal. (3.2, 3.8)

6. Do you want _____ ice cream? (3.2)

7. Do you want _____ ice cream cone? (1.3, 3.1)

8. There are _____ interesting people in my class. (3.2)

9. I like _____ movies about mysteries. (3.2)

10. Jack had _____ egg on his tie. (3.8)

ANSWERS

1. an
2. a
3. an, a
4. an
5. θ

6. θ
7. an
8. θ
9. θ
10. θ

Number correct: _____ out of 11.

REVIEW EXERCISE THREE

Write **a,** or **an** only where they are needed. Write θ where no article is needed.

1. Jack's father is _____ professor at Boston University. (4.1)

2. His mother is _____ engineer. (4.1)

3. I want to be _____ pilot. (4.1)

4. Pilots can earn $45,000 _____ year. (4.2)

5. Mr. Zac is always grumpy and unpleasant. As a result, he has _____ few friends. (4.5)

6. I've been saving all year, so I have _____ little money. It's enough to buy a second-hand car. (4.5)

7. California is the kind of _____ place I'd like to go on vacation. (4.4)

8. It's _____ shame that you can't come to my party. (4.3)

9. Southerners never seem to be in _____ rush the way New Yorkers are. (4.3)

10. She is _____ excellent teacher. (4.1)

11. I brush my teeth twice _____ day. (4.2)

12. Quite _____ few people like tennis. (4.5)

13. Henry is the type of _____ man that everyone likes. (4.4)

14. Are you in _____ good mood today? (4.3)

ANSWERS

1. a		8. a	
2. an		9. a	
3. a		10. an	
4. a		11. a	
5. θ		12. a	
6. a		13. θ	
7. θ		14. a	

Number correct: _____ out of 14

REVIEW EXERCISE FOUR

Write *a, an,* or *the* in the sentences below:

1. For my birthday I received _____ book and _____ umbrella. (3.1, 5.2)

2. _____ book was from Aunt Mary and _____ umbrella was from Uncle Tom. (5.1)

3. We couldn't see because _____ lights went out. (5.2)

4. _____ sky is overcast today. I think it will rain. (5.3)

5. We watched _____ moon rise over the mountain. (5.3)

6. Sue is _____ good cook. As a matter of fact, she is _____ best cook I know. (4.1, 5.5)

7. Moby Dick is _____ interesting book. It's _____ best book I've ever read. (1.3, 5.5)

ANSWERS

1. a, an
2. The, the
3. the
4. The

5. the
6. a, the
7. an, the

Number correct: _____ out of 11

REVIEW EXERCISE FIVE:

Write *the* only where it is needed. Write θ where no article is needed.

1. _____ monkeys are smarter than _____ dogs. (6.1)

2. _____ women in my family are all short. (6.1)

3. I like _____ fresh fruits and _____ vegetables. (6.1)

4. Everyone loves _____ clowns. (6.1)

5. _____ clowns in Ringling Brothers' Circus are _____ funniest clowns in _____ world. (6.1, 5.5, 5.3)

6. _____ Sunday is the first day of the week. (6.2)

7. I'll see you _____ Tuesday at 4 o'clock. (6.2)

8. Will you be home for _____ Christmas? (6.2)

9. America's birthday is _____ Fourth of July. (6.3)

10. Children in school are excited on _____ Friday before vacation begins. (6.4)

11. I read a story about _____ Richard _____ Lionhearted. (6.9)

12. _____ Mr. Jones is our teacher. (6.5)

13. _____ Smiths have been our neighbors for a long time. (6.7)

14. Have you ever seen _____ Adams Family on television? (6.8)

15. The treaty was signed by _____ King George. (6.5)

ANSWERS

1. θ, θ	6. θ	11. θ, the
2. The	7. θ	12. θ
3. θ, θ	8. θ	13. The
4. θ	9. the	14. the
5. The, the, the	10. the	15. θ

Number right: _____ out of 20

REVIEW EXERCISE SIX

Write **a, an, the,** or *my, his,* or *her.*

1. I have _____ headache. (6.11)

2. I accidentally poked myself in _____ eye. (6.11)

3. Frank hurt _____ hand when he caught the ball. (6.10)

4. She washed _____ face with warm water and soap. (6.10)

5. The ball hit me in _____ head. (6.11)

6. The policeman was shot in _____ shoulder. (6.11)

7. The little boy got dirt on _____ shirt. (6.10)

Write *the* where it is needed. Write θ where no article is needed.

8. _____ milk comes from _____ cows. (7.1, 3.2)

9. _____ milk in this glass is sour. (7.4)

10. _____ chocolate milk is delicious. (7.2, 7.3)

11. Some people will do anything for _____ money. (7.2)

12. I enjoy _____ literature of the Middle Ages. (7.5)

13. _____ literature was my favorite subject in school. (7.6)

14. Do you like _____ music of Mozart? (7.5)

15. Everyone likes _____ music. (7.6)

16. Someday there will be an end to _____ war. (7.7)

17. Someday there will be an end to _____ war in Nicaragua. (7.5)

18. Charlie has been studying _____ Italian for two years. (7.6)

19. _____ Italian spoken in Rome is different from _____ Italian spoken in Naples. (7.5)

ANSWERS:

1. a	11. θ
2. the	12. the
3. his	13. θ
4. her	14. the
5. the	15. θ
6. the	16. θ
7. his	17. the
8. θ, θ	18. θ
9. The	19. The, the
10. θ	

Number right: _____ out of 20

REVIEW EXERCISE SEVEN

Write *a* or *the* where they are needed. Write θ where no article is needed.

1. Mr. Jackson had _____ bad heart, and _____ high blood pressure. (7.9, 7.8)

2. She had _____ stomach ache, but it was not _____ appendicitis. (7.9, 7.8)

3. Bob caught _____ mumps from Kelly. (7.9)

4. You can get a vaccination against _____ measles, and _____ polio. (7.9, 7.8)

5. Laura had _____ fever of 100.2 degrees. (7.9)

6. Dr. Wheeler plays _____ piano very well. (7.10)

7. She also studied _____ violin. (7.10)

8. Do you enjoy _____ mathematics? (7.11)

9. We play _____ bridge every Sunday afternoon. (7.11)

10. My brother plays _____ soccer. (7.11)

ANSWERS:

1. a, θ	6. the
2. a, θ	7. the
3. the	8. θ
4. the, θ	9. θ
5. a	10. θ

Number right: _____ out of 13

REVIEW EXERCISE EIGHT

Write *the* only where it is needed. Write θ where no article is needed.

1. Everyone goes to _____ bed early at our house. (7.12)

2. _____ bed in the hotel we stayed at was very comfortable. (7.12)

3. What time does _____ school begin? (7.12)

4. I go to _____ church on Sundays. (7.12)

5. _____ Australia, _____ Europe, and _____ Africa are continents. (8.1)

6. We went to _____ Lake Louise for our vacation. (8.1)

7. _____ Great Lakes are _____ largest fresh water lakes in America. (8.2, 5.5)

8. _____ Alps are in _____ Austria and _____ Switzerland. (8.2, 8.1)

9. _____ Soviet Union and _____ People's Republic of China are two greatworld powers. (8.3)

10. Her house was on _____ Twenty-ninth Street. (8.1)

11. _____ Everglades is a swamp in _____ Florida. (8.2, 8.1)

12. _____ Canada is north of _____ United States. (8.1, 8.3)

13. _____ Bronx is one of the boroughs of _____ New York City. (8.1, 8.4)

14. _____ Sixth Avenue is called _____ Avenue of the Americas in Midtown Manhattan. (8.1, 8.6)

15. _____ Hague is the capital of _____ Netherlands. (8.4, 8.2)

ANSWERS

1. θ	9. The, the
2. The	10. θ
3. θ	11. The, θ
4. θ	12. θ, the
5. θ, θ, θ	13. The, θ
6. θ	14. θ, The
7. The, the	15. The, The
8. The, θ, θ	

Number right: _____ out of 26

REVIEW EXERCISE NINE

Write *the* where it is needed. Write θ where no article is needed.

1. _____ Golden Gate Bridge connects _____ San Francisco with _____ Marin County. (8.7, 8.1)

2. _____ Gulf of Mexico is _____ south of _____ Texas. (8.7, 8.9, 8.1)

3. _____ Missouri River flows into _____ Mississippi River. (8.7)

4. I'm from _____ South. (8.8)

5. _____ Mexico is bounded by _____ Pacific Ocean on _____ west, _____ United States on _____ north, _____ Gulf of Mexico on _____ east, and _____ Guatemala on _____ south. (8.1, 8.7, 8.8)

6. Italy is _____ south of Switzerland. (8.9)

7. Karen went to _____ Harvard, while her sister went to _____ University of Indiana. (8.10, 8.11)

8. While we were in Washington, D.C., we visited _____ White House, _____ Lincoln Memorial, and _____ Smithsonian Museum. (8.11)

ANSWERS

1. The, θ, θ
2. The, θ, θ
3. The, the
4. the
5. θ, the, the, the
   the, the, the, θ, the

6. θ
7. θ, the
8. the, the, the

Number right: _____ out of 24.

REVIEW EXERCISE TEN

Write *the* where it is needed. Write θ where no article is needed.

1. My favorite magazines are _____ Time, _____ Newsweek, and _____ Life. (9.3)

2. The boss reads two newspapers a day: _____ New York Times and _____ Wall Street Journal. (9.4)

3. We like to shop at _____ Bloomingdales or _____ Macy's. (9.1)

4. _____ Renaissance began in Italy during _____ fourteenth century. (9.5)

5. What was _____ first job you held when you graduated college? (9.6)

6. I've told you for _____ hundredth time, don't exaggerate! (9.6)

7. _____ first and second chapters were hard, but by the time I got to _____ Chapter Ten, I understood everything. (9.6, 9.9)

8. December is _____ last month of the year. (9.6)

9. I went to visit him _____ last month. (9.7)

10. Do you believe in love at _____ first sight? (9.8)

ANSWERS

1. θ, θ, θ	6. the
2. The, The	7. the, θ
3. θ, θ	8. the
4. The, the	9. θ
5. the	10. θ

Number right: _____ out of 16.

MASTERY TEST

PART I Write **a**, **an** or **the** where they are needed. Write θ where no article is needed.

1. I like _____ rice.

2. _____ cats are good mouse hunters.

3. Juliana used to play _____ guitar.

4. We saw _____ fattest lady in _____ world at the circus last week.

5. _____ Bob plays _____ tennis very well.

6. _____ water is _____ best drink when you are thirsty.

7. Please put the pillow on _____ bed.

8. I don't go to _____ school on _____ Sunday.

9. There was an accident in front of _____ church.

10. I wrote a long letter to _____ O'Briens.

11. We need _____ oxygen to breathe.

12. _____ sugar in this bowl is full of lumps.

13. What is _____ worst thing that ever happened to you?

14. _____ love is a beautiful emotion.

15. Frank studied _____ history at _____ college.

16. What time do you go to _____ bed?

17. _____ school is on the corner.

18. I think that _____ mathematics is _____ hardest subject in school.

19. _____ seals are very good swimmers.

20. I don't like _____ dresses in this store.

21. When I spoke about Bill Martin, I meant _____ Bill Martin who lives in Cliffside Park, not _____ Bill Martin from Englewood.

58

22. Do you like _____ American food?

23. _____ stars are shining brightly.

24. _____ Lake Michigan is one of _____ Great Lakes.

25. Most people hate _____ war.

26. Ed wants to be _____ composer.

27. She earns seven dollars _____ hour at her part-time job.

28. I heard the news on _____ radio.

29. We see Frank four or five times _____ week.

30. You seem to be in _____ good mood.

31. There is _____ little hope that the police will find the thieves. They left no clues.

32. Sam is always in _____ hurry.

33. Many _____ tear has to fall in the game of love and romance.

34. I found _____ wallet and a keychain. _____ wallet was empty but it
    had _____ identification card in it.

35. It's _____ beautiful day today. _____ sky is blue and _____ sun is shining.
    _____ weather is perfect.

36. Last night _____ moon rose at seven p.m.

37. We went to visit _____ Smiths.

38. Leif _____ Lucky was the Viking who discovered America.

39. I have _____ headache.

40. Bob bumped himself on _____ head.

41. We were worried about _____ disappearance of our dog.

42. Doctors are hoping to find a cure for _____ cancer.

43. Patty had _____ fever of 103 degrees when she had _____ mumps.

44. Let's play _____ baseball after school.

45. Barbara practices _____ piano for two hours every day.

46. What time do you go to _____ bed?

47. The thief spent five years in _____ prison.

48. _____ Central Park Zoo is on _____ Fifth Avenue.

49. We stayed at _____ Plaza Hotel.

50. _____ Mexico is south of _____ United States.

ANSWERS

1. θ	14. θ	27. an	40. the
2. θ	15. θ, θ	28. the	41. the
3. the	16. θ	29. a	42. θ
4. the, the	17. The	30. a	43. a, the
5. θ, θ	18. θ, the	31. θ	44. θ
6. θ, the	19. θ	32. a	45. the
7. the	20. the	33. a	46. θ
8. θ, θ	21. the, the	34. a, The, an	47. θ
9. the	22. θ	35. a, The, the, The	48. The, θ
10. the	23. The	36. the	49. the
11. θ	24. θ, the	37. the	50. θ, The
12. The	25. θ	38. the	
13. the	26. a	39. a	

Number correct: _____ out of 65.

PART II Answer these questions in complete sentences. Have a native-English speaking person correct them.

1. Where are you from?

_____

2. What street do you live on?

_____

3. What subjects do you enjoy?

_____

4. Do you play any musical instruments? What are they?

_____

5. What games and sports do you play?

   _____

6. What did you eat for lunch yesterday?

   _____

7. What language do you speak?

   _____

8. What time do you go to bed?

   _____

9. Have you ever traveled? Where to?

   _____

10. What museums have you visited?

    _____

11. What famous places have you seen?

    _____

12. What section of the country are you from?

    _____

13. What countries border your country?

    _____

14. What rivers and mountains are in your country?

    _____

15. What animals do you like?

    _____

16. What newspapers and magazines do you read?

    _____

17. What school or college did you go to?

    _____

18. Who would you call to report an accident?

    _____

19. Who is your favorite movie star?

    _____

20. What century is this?

    _____

21. Where do you buy your food?

_____

22. What time do you go to bed?

_____

23. What illnesses have you had?

_____

24. What do you put on your hamburger before you eat it?

_____

25. What day is your birthday?

_____

PART III Write or tell the story of The Wild Dog and the Farm Dog in your own words.

_____

_____

_____

_____

_____

_____

_____

_____

_____

_____

_____

_____

_____